"Mike, you missed your calling, you are most definitely a comedian. Thank you for sharing in this life journey daily and keeping the veil lifted. You are awesome. I love you."

"I've subscribed to lots of these things and they lose their charge, start to get repetitive, etc. But I have to hand it to you, Mike—you keep me hoppin' and I just LOVE IT! WHAT A BLAST this is—definitely sounds like you're talkin' just to me."

"I receive messages from other best-selling spiritual gurus on the internet, but your messages are the most profound, heartwarming, everyday-commonsense, take-it-with-you, mind-uplifting, and unselfish messages received. THANK YOU, Mike! Blessings to you and your good work."

"I used to REALLY, REALLY look forward to weekends. But since I started receiving the daily Notes from the Universe on Monday through Friday, weekends are not such a big deal now. I even look forward to coming back to work on Monday, since I know that I will feel loved and valued because of the Universe. Kind of makes me realize what's really important in life . . . at least in my life. Thanks for all of the encouragement. I couldn't make it without you."

"You may not have my faith in Jesus or in the Holy Spirit or in God as my Heavenly Loving Father, but, nevertheless, your Notes from the Universe are helping me live the Covenant Spiritual Life I have been wanting to live for a very long time. I just thought you would like to know this, and I wanted to say THANK YOU for helping me to bring Glory to my Lord."

"I don't know if you know it or not, but to some of us out here your messages are vitally important, that consistent light that helps guide and strengthen faith to keep us going and give us courage to reach further and to strive toward spiritual growth and happiness—toward a more meaningful and fulfilling life. You are doing such a wonderful and thoughtful thing for so many of us, I just wanted to say thank you!! Eternally grateful."

"Thank you, Mike. You may never know how much this note means to me today, but I do hope that my gratitude will in some way reach you and bless your life in ways that make even a bright light like you stop and go WOW!"

"For several years I've enjoyed your messages and they never fail to touch my heart. Thanks so much, Mike, for all you do for everyone and, yes, especially for me. I feel like your messages come to me with heartfelt sincerity . . . and I won't even ask you, 'How DO you do it?' You are obviously well connected. Thanks again."

"I appreciate your messages. They are like golden nuggets that bless and inspire me. 'Thank you' is an understatement, but I must say it anyway: Thank you."

Even More Notes from the Universe

DANCING LIFE'S DANCE

Mike Dooley

ATRIA BOOKS
New York London Toronto Sydney

BEYOND WORDS
Hillsboro, Oregon

ATRIA BOOKS
A Division of Simon & Schuster, Inc.
1230 Avenue of the Americas
New York, NY 10020

BEYOND WORDS
20827 N.W. Cornell Road, Suite 500
Hillsboro, Oregon 97124-9808
503-531-8700 / 503-531-8773 fax
www.beyondword.com

First Atria Books/Beyond Words hardcover edition November 2008

ATRIA BOOKS and colophon are trademarks of Simon & Schuster, Inc.

Beyond Words Publishing is a division of Simon & Schuster, Inc.

For more information about special discounts for bulk purchases,
please contact Simon & Schuster Special Sales at
1-800-456-6798 or business@simonandschuster.com.

Manufactured in the United States of America

1 3 5 7 9 10 8 6 4 2

Library of Congress Cataloging-in-Publication Data

Dooley, Mike.

Even more notes from the universe: dancing life's dance / Mike Dooley.
p.   cm.
1. Self-help techniques—Miscellanea. 2. Spirituality—Miscellanea.
3. Occultism—Miscellanea. I. Title.
BF1999.D61551   2008
158—dc22   2008017876

ISBN-13: 978-1-58270-186-8
ISBN-10:   1-58270-186-5

The corporate mission of Beyond Words Publishing, Inc.: *Inspire to Integrity*

For Dad

INTRODUCTION

When asked what you do for a living, do you squirm, fidget, or evade? I do. I write Notes from the Universe for a living and I send them to e-mail subscribers five days a week, for free. Doesn't quite have the same ring as doctor, lawyer, or accountant, even butcher, baker, or candlestick maker. And it never quite impresses the way I once thought it might.

Nevertheless, writing for the Universe has taught me a number of things about myself and the creative process, and for this third installment of the trilogy, I thought I'd share a little of it, as these lessons have a number of applications to the rest of my life, and perhaps will to yours as well.

First, I'm better than I usually give myself credit for. There's hardly been a time in the past eight years when I consistently felt that I've been writing well, or as well as I could. In fact, more often than not, I've felt like I was in a slump. But every now and then a funny thing happens. For some reason or other I have to rummage through the old archives, and lo . . . I can't seem to find when the last lull was, as I'm quite impressed with what I read.

Interestingly, and I hate to admit this, I'll then think, "Wow, I wish I were writing like that now!" Only to discover, several months later, that I actually was. And this has gone on for quite some time, perpetually feeling like today's creativity pales compared to yesterday's.

However slow I've been to learn my lesson, I really *have* been paying attention. In writing, just as in all areas of my life, I'm usually much better than I give myself credit for at the time, and I'm quite sure you are, too.

Second, just because I don't know what I'm going to write doesn't mean I shouldn't start. Inspiration to write, or to do anything else, usually comes *after*, not *before*, we physically begin the journey—no matter what kind of journey it is. Don't wait for your ducks to line up first because they never do, not until you start. Even a momma duck knows this. Her ducklings are hither and yon until she *starts* her journey, at which point they scramble to catch up and fall in line. The same is true of our own ducks.

And last, happy and joyful thoughts physically change the material world. My creative process for writing is modeled after what I share with audiences for manifesting change in their lives. First, define and imagine what you want *in terms of the end result*, preferably emotionally. Second, take action toward that end result to ramp-up belief in your success and to put yourself in a place of receivership for the manifestation.

For step one, I visualize for a minute or two before each writing session. In my mind, *I feel the joy*. Physically, I pump my fists, wave my palms, and let out a loud, "Whooooohooooooo . . ." and whatnot.

Step two comes by typing the first words that pop into my mind once I finish visualizing. This is a bit challenging, since often those words don't make much sense, nor will they necessarily be used, but I've found that by physically taking action toward the vision I imagine, the ideas, creativity, and insights I need eventually burst forth. This is very simply because the *end result* I put forth (feeling joy) cannot *physically* become real unless I write really well. And I cannot write really well without such bursts of divine inspiration.

In the end, I'm physically whooping up a storm

because before my very eyes I've witnessed thoughts becoming things in the form of word combinations and sentences that have never before existed, to be sent out as an e-mail, later to be bound into a book, and, finally, to be reflected in smiles on faces all over the world, even long after my time in space has come and gone. And this is exactly the kind of tangible difference your own happiness can make, whether or not you write.

Still, these days, more often than not, I tell enquiring minds that "I do a little writing, I do a little speaking . . ." and politely change the subject.

To the life of *your* dreams,

HOW YOU MIGHT
USE THIS BOOK

When these Notes were first sent out by e-mail to subscribers, the most common reply I received (and still receive, endlessly) was that more often than not, day after day, readers were amazed by the uncanny timing of each Note as it related to exactly where they were in their respective lives. "How could you know? Even my closest friends don't have a clue!" or "I was eating French toast at 4 a.m. when today's Note arrived . . . and I *had* to call and wake my mother to share that the PS asked, 'More syrup?' just as I was reaching for it!" or "As I was worrying about the sad ending of my marriage and its potential effect on my children, tears and tissues everywhere, today's Note arrived telling me, 'If you only knew just how incredibly well everything is going to turn out, for you and those close to you, right now you'd likely feel light as a feather, free as the wind, happy, confident, giddy . . .'"

How, indeed? The obvious answer is that while 250,000 people receive the exact same Note, they each interpret it 250,000 different ways, filtered through their own thoughts and circumstances. The not-so-obvious answer is that in the jungles of time and space, things are *not* as they appear. We've been told since our lives began that we are but mere bystanders to the glory of life and that everything happens along a rigid, linear time line. The truth, however, is that we're each the co-creator of all that we share, and our experiences spring from an eternal now. It's only our exclusive reliance upon our physical senses to interpret life that makes this notion so challenging to grasp. And so, just as those who witness a beautiful sunrise actually participate in its creation, so, too, in some mystical, magical way are the readers of these words and the daily Notes their co-creators—whether they were received as an e-mail in the "past" or randomly chosen from the pages now before you.

Go on, give it a try. Just open this book to any "random" page and see what you get. You're really quite the writer, you know.

*Can you imagine an astral plane
somewhere "out there"*
where very old souls could rendezvous to practice and
perfect their most highly developed manifestation
techniques? A members-only kind of place, where
whatever they think about comes to life in the most
vivid high-definition, surround sound Technicolor,
vis-à-vis the most intricate plots and circumstances?
Where the only limits that exist lie in their ability to
imagine what they have never before imagined, and to
move with it in anticipation of its "physical" expression?

And best of all, being astral, no harm can come to them.
They're completely untouchable. Nothing is real, yet
everything matters. And there can be infinite gains in
terms of insight and fun, yet no losses since everything is
illusory. Actually, the worst thing that can happen is
that they temporarily become so entranced by their
creations, they completely forget who they are, where
they are, and how powerful they really are.

Yep, it would be exactly like this astral plane.
Only here, to help wake 'em up from their trance,
we're experimenting with Notes from the Universe . . .

Notes

from the

Universe

To clarify "eternal"
just a smidge . . .

Once the river of time has rounded her
final bend, and the last star in the sky has
brightened its last night, and every child
who may ever be conceived has been
given ten thousand names . . .
we will have just begun.

Got time?

*When I think of how much you
and I have to look forward to,
I almost hyperventilate.*

1

Want to know what's better
than having it all? Way, way better?

Not having it all, but knowing
of its inevitability, in a never-ending
adventure that's just barely begun.

Yeeeeeehaaaaaaaaaaaaaaaa!

*Kind of like Friday
just before the weekend.*

It never fails to amaze me.

Create a paradise out of the ether. Throw in some wildlife, volcanoes, and windstorms. Some iguanas, koalas, and waterfalls. Come back a few billion years later, and just when it looks like the whole place is going to implode—with pollution, disease, and war; famine, fatigue, and fright—there are still those who see the beauty. Who act with kindness. And who live with hope and gratitude.

Actually, they carry the entire planet.
Who'd have thunk?

Yeah, okay. Guilty.

By the simple act of thinking, vortexes are created, invisible energies are applied, and circumstances begin creeping to make real what was previously just imagined. This supernatural pull of your thoughts continues long after you think them, whenever there follows intent, expectation, and action; moving mountains, parting rivers, and doing the "impossible" until there is the inevitable manifestation.

This is how your "thoughts become things." How they physically become things in a dimension that already exists, with billions of players and massive momentum. Not by appearing out of thin air, but through a manipulation of forces in the unseen that literally begin shifting, morphing, and rearranging all of the elements in your life so as to deliver to you the nearest equivalent of what you've been thinking. In other words, the "law of attraction."

"Thoughts become things" explains the law of attraction. It's why there is a law of attraction. And unlike any other three words in all the vocabularies of all the languages in all the world, "thoughts become things" tells you exactly where you fit into the picture, as the thinker, the decision maker over what you will think about, revealing your power as a supernatural, all-powerful, unlimited CREATOR.

But, of course, many prefer not to think of themselves as so phenomenally powerful.

I should have shared this earlier,
but, well, I'm the Universe and I've been busy.

In the beginning, long before there were even
beaches to walk along, clouds to float upon,
or stars to wish on, I dreamed of you and
your happiness.

And everything that has
ever been added since was to that end.

*See? You are so much more to me
than just pretty planet decoration.*

Do you know
what "unlimited" means?

It means you decide—*everything*.

Without a doubt,
right here and now, as you read these
very words with eyes that sparkle,
this golden day, amid your dancing
manifestations in a perfect world on an
emerald planet while your heart beats,
your blood flows, and angels peer over
your shoulder, I think you just might be
the luckiest person alive.

The best way to find "love,"
which, incidentally, is just as true
for finding money, is to focus less on these
by-products of a life well lived and more on
a life well lived.

Simple is as simple does.

Dance life's dance, today, without preconditions.

Ain't it grand?

Doesn't it boggle your mind? The harmony,
the splendor, the beauty. The intricacies,
the synchronicities, the staggering perfection.
Do you ever wonder how it all came about?

Do you think I studied quarks, atoms, and
molecules? That I drew schematics for the sun,
the moon, and the stars; the otter, the Gila
monster, and the penguin? Do you think I
painted every zebra, flower, and butterfly?

Or, do you think,
I simply imagined the end result?

And that's all you ever have to do.

Sheez, I thought you knew I hated school.

Do you think you're going to feel cheated
on the day you discover that your countless
successes were pretty much inevitable?
And that all the doubts, the fretting,
and the worries were a silly waste of time?
Or do you think you'll just roll with
things . . . carefree . . . blissful . . . and with
a permanent catlike smile on your face?

Yeah. Roll, and the other stuff.
That's what we said you'd do.

So . . . how about it?

A-one, and a-two . . .
Meow, meow, meow, meow . . .
Meow, meow, meow, meow . . .

The Universe, and all her proud felines.

To set the record straight:
However cool you think it might be to have an
out-of-body experience—floating over your house,
flying through space, traversing the past, present,
and future—let me tell you, it'll never be as cool
as being in the one you have now. Walking
barefoot in the grass, floating in a sun-drenched
pool, and dancing alone in the dark.

You so "fly,"
The Universe

*Trust me, from here, getting into-body
is considered the most sacred of all sacreds.*

I hope you're loving your life.
And I do mean really, really loving your life.

Because right now there are so many others
who are (loving your life). In time and space,
and in the unseen.

*No, not all of them will admit it, but I know these
things, and one day they'll know them, too.*

I gotta confess,

every now and then I get this incredible urge
to splurge on myself. To really indulge. Pull out
all the stops. And tickle every one of my senses.

Yep, and that's when I'll choose a lifetime like
yours. With obstacles to challenge me, people to
"test" me, and circumstances that force me to see
things that even I have never seen before. And a
personality like yours, which possesses faith so
daring that even when lost, you still hope. Dreams
so bold that even when you fall, you get back up.
And a heart so big that even when it breaks,
as all big hearts do, there's always room for
second chances and new romances.

That's what I do.

Talk about crazy, sexy, and cool!

The Universe

Thanks.

Whoops . . . I did it again.

Took a little nap, had a few dreams, and worlds were born. Planets spun and cooled. Continents rose and fell. And civilizations clashed and united.

Actually, it's quite good fun. But I also dreamed I was you. And in that dream, for a spell, I didn't remember I was also the Universe.

It was frightful, actually. Just about scared me to death until, as you, I slowly remembered who I was. And in those waking moments, it was as if the earth shook, the seas danced, and the skies rejoiced almost as much as myself. As if they were waking up, too. It was the most beautiful, sublime, intoxicating rush of pure joy I think I've ever known.

How I wish I could tell you more.
But like a farmer eager for the new crop,
any rush to harvest would spoil the yield.
Besides, words would utterly fail me.

The sad part
is that they told you it's wrong to be selfish,
tacky to be vain, vulgar to be sexy,
and wasteful to be rich.

The happy part is that they were
just making all that up.

Probably just jealous of all you might do,
be, and have. And afraid of all they might not.

Uh-oh . . .
One of them is in trouble now, gotta bolt!

Sometimes, when what they said
or promised doesn't match what they did,
and what they did, to this day, still hurts,
you're better off forgetting all about it . . .
knowing that I won't.

I'm like an elephant.

Okay, for just five minutes
forget the bucks. Forget your soul mate, too.
Forget the new car, the "home run," and being
on *Oprah*. Forget your fears, your problems,
and your pain. And during those five minutes,
feel the feelings you most want to feel,
for the rest of your life.

It might seem awkward, that's okay.
It might seem silly, too. And I can just about
guarantee, at first, it'll feel utterly futile . . . until
your entire life begins to change.

If I were a beggar, I'd beg you. If I prayed in question
marks, this is what I'd ask for. And if I could implore

you to do anything, let this be it. Because nothing else that you might ever do will have as profound an effect on your fortunes, friendships, and happiness; in navigating the illusions, manifesting what you want, and avoiding what you dread; as this little five-minute drill performed just once a day, on as many days as you remember to do it.

And just so you know, if you do this right now or even every day for the rest of your life, I'll add back those five minutes to each of the days you do it. I'll just sneak 'em in there, and they'll feel like ten.

But . . . not a word to anyone.

And that reminds me,
since I don't pray in question marks,
I hope you don't, either.

You know, "Can I, please . . . ? Will you,
please . . . ? If I do X, or sacrifice Y,
will you do Z . . . ?" We have spam
filters here, too, and since only you can
answer those questions, they kind of just
go in one port and out the other.

But, hubba-hubba, if you pray in "thank-yous,"
especially for stuff you haven't yet received
or experienced (but as if you already had),
those we all hear.

Amen!

The Universe

It took some craftiness

to create the splendors you now live in,
because it all had to be done with the most
exquisite balance, and in just such a way
that you'd never, ever become bored.

Yeah, I had to throw in a few valleys so that you
could truly appreciate the peaks. A few scaly, ugly,
biting creatures, to make the others more adorable.
Some slippery slopes, dangerous curves, and moving
targets, to show you how agile, brilliant, and
cunning you are. And some quicksand, tornadoes,
and earthquakes, to help you appreciate a stolen
nap, an evening stroll, and quiet times.

But perhaps, best of all, I had to dream up some
pretty special people. You know, with perspectives
and traits so unlike your own that sometimes it
would seem your only means of surviving the
relationship would be learning to love yourself,
even more. Aren't they a piece of work?

Oh, the sublime irony.

Phew . . . I need a break!
Tell you what, why don't you write
your own Note today? To me?

You could say something like, "Jambo Universe,
it's me! Right, the good-looking, talented,
sexy one for whom the sun rises every day.
Anyway, just wanted to tell you that this
adventure in time and space has been awesome.
Everything I ever expected it would be. (Huh,
imagine that.) It's been exactly as hard and
as easy, as challenging and as rewarding, as I've
been telling myself. (Hey, what a coincidence.)
And even though I know we are ONE, I still like
thinking of you "out there" somewhere,

watching, loving, and protecting me. (Hmm, could this also be why I sometimes feel alone?) At any rate, I'm learning tons, having some fun, and really looking forward to coming home one day. (Unless, of course, I'm home now.)

Hey, since I have your attention, thanks for another day in paradise. (Where my thoughts become things, dreams never stop coming true, and it all just keeps getting better and better.)

You never cease to amaze me.

23

Next time you feel really hurt,
really angry, or really, really upset,
and you're sure that even I have been violated,
shaken, and humbled, quick, check and see
if the sky is any less blue, the sun any less
radiant, the birds have stopped singing,
or the flowers have lost their scent.

I'll wager you'll find that life has gone on much
as before. Too consumed by the powers of now
and the inevitabilities of love, understanding,
and eternal life to have even missed a beat.

Oh-wee-oh,

The Universe

That's if there even is a next time.

"Grasshopper,"

you may not always know what your invisible, limiting beliefs are. But you do always know the kinds of empowering beliefs you'd like to possess. And so, one decision at a time, one day at a time, you can choose to behave accordingly. And thereby effectively kick some wicked, limiting-belief butt.

For every decision, crossroad, or act of faith, choose with the mind of the highest within you. Until that's all there is.

There's *always* another way.

Always.

It takes a *really* special person,
someone quite extraordinary, to find true
happiness in the lap of luxury surrounded by
wealth and abundance, friends and laughter,
and choices, choices, choices.

And funnily enough, it's usually the exact
same kind of person who can be happy
without all that, spending time alone,
maybe with a book, or some tools, or a dog
for the odd distraction.

Get my drift?

For every fork in the road,
there are often two paths from which
to choose . . . the one you "should" take
and the one you want to take.

Take the second.
Always take the second.

I did.

*Man, could life rock
any more than it does?*

There hasn't been one
single day of your life when the world
hasn't been made a better place
by your presence in it.

If you only knew.

Just do what you can
with what's before you today . . .
and leave "spectacular" to me.

'Kay?

The same goes for "profound," "stellar,"
"revolutionary," and "outrageous."

When you tough it out,
hold the line, and stay the course,
I promise you there will soon come a day
when you look back over your shoulder,
shake your head in dismay, and seriously
wonder what all the fuss was about.

Just like all the other times.

*In fact, in not so many days from today,
it will become clear as a bell that you did
have enough time, that you were never alone,
and that all of us in the unseen were working
double time to help make possible
"the time of your life."*

Yeeeeehaaaaaaaaaaaaaaa! XOXOXO.

It was such a sad, sad picture.
She cried and cried, and ever so
faintly murmured, "Oh, how I wish you
were here with me now . . . That you
could have always been with me . . .
That we could have lived forever."

And so I whispered into her ear so softly
that my words could only be felt, not heard,
"He is, he will be, and you do."

She'll see.

Never trust appearances.

Can you hear it?
The entire Kingdom now beckons.

There were no tests,
no hoops, and no limits.

All I have, I press to you
at this very moment.

This is all you have to know.

And all you have to do is make room
for the torrent that will flow in direct
proportion to your every preparation,
including what you do today.

You mean the world to me.

You know, a kind word
can move mountains and change lives.
But for those times when they've escaped you,
when the right thing wasn't said, and the time
wasn't right to say it, kind thoughts can do
the same. And better, thoughts have a way
of lingering, seeking, and finding their intended
beneficiary, unfettered by time and space.
So it's never too late to think 'em,
nor are you ever too far away.

Just a little something a tree once told me.

Guess who's thinking of you, right now?

Has it occurred to you
that wherever you go, you are my eyes,
my ears, and my voice; my arms, my legs,
and my everything else, too?

Well, I vote for more flowers, more music,
and more "I love yous." More hugging,
more skipping, and more naps.

But that's just me.

XXXXXXXXXXXOOOOOOOOOOO!

TOGA! TOGA! TOGA!

What, you think the Universe
doesn't have toga parties?

Believe me, here it never ends!

The homecoming parties are really crazy!
Old loves and friendships are rekindled and
spontaneous enlightenment is passed around like,
well, like you know what. But then, there are
the after parties . . . whoooeeee! Real hoedowns
for the most brilliant, radiant, and illuminated
souls in our midst. Fearless beings willing to
further the collective consciousness by delving
into a kaleidoscope of emotions. Embarking
upon the greatest adventure ever imagined into
the sacred, hallowed jungles of time and space,
where illumination is taken to dazzling new levels
and salvation guaranteed, not for what they might
do with their lives, but for simply seeing them
through. The Bon Voyage parties.

We owe you BIG.

If you just start dancing,
I can assure you, by the powers vested in me
(more than you could ever imagine),
the music will be added. As will the partners,
the giant disco ball, and whatever else you like.

But I must warn you, "start" is not to be
confused with "start, and then stop to see if
anything happens." Nope, that's "I'm scared,
tired, and not sure of what I really want."

I mean "start" as in "never stop,
never look back, because even if I've made
a 'mistake,' at least I still get to dance."

Do your thing, and I'll do mine.

Cha, cha, cha.

If you know what you want,
and you can remember that "thoughts
become things" is the only absolute law
at play in time and space, what else matters
but what you choose to think today?

Banzai!

The thing that most forget
while dreamily looking off into the horizon
for the ship of their dreams is that such
ships never sail in but are actually built
beneath their very feet.

Get my drift?

I keep telling 'em

that it's a jungle out there; that time and space isn't a place for "scaredies"; that toes are stubbed, hearts are broken, and dreams can seem to be shattered into a million pieces. I tell 'em that the illusions are so captivating, they won't even remember who they really are. And that the emotions can be so painful, at times they might fleetingly wish they were dead.

But it's like, that just makes them want to go even more.

Adventurers.

You bad.

What part of "visualize"
do you think most people misunderstand?

Or don't they do it, just once a day,
for five minutes a day, because they've yet
to realize that whatever it is they most want
lies only a little thinking away?

"Can you hear me now?"

*Just once a day, for five minutes a day,
followed by a little "preparing the way," and you,
too, could sing like Madonna, golf like Tiger,
and waltz like Matilda.*

You know that feeling,

when all of a sudden it seems like everything
you ever wanted to happen starts happening
at once. And you're totally blown away, on top of
the world, almost feeling like you don't even have
any more dreams because they're all coming true.
Yet you're slammed because you're stretching
yourself like you've never stretched before, just
trying to keep up with them. And every day some
new magical realization hits you! And you've never
felt so happy in your life. Except that you wish
so badly that everyone close to you could have the
same overwhelming experiences, the same sensory
overload. And more, you wish everyone on the
planet could feel it, too, at least just a little,
because it's so intoxicating. And you feel like you
now understand all the tough times, and all the
slow days, and all the phases when it seemed like
absolutely nothing was happening in your life.

And you wonder why you haven't always felt like this because what you feel is so much more than just the joy of dreams coming true. It's like you're feeling the heartbeat of everyone's life at once. And you realize there's always been so much more to be happy about than sad. And you wonder what it was that used to trouble you, and how it could have seemed so real, or how it could've seemed bigger than the beauty you now face. And you just shake your head, knowing how perfect everything is, how perfect it's always been, and how perfect it will always be. And you give thanks with your hands over your face, tasting the salt of your tears, and you know that this, this feeling, more than anything else you've ever experienced, was so meant to be.

Well, this is just a tiny, little taste of what it feels like to be the Universe, at all times.

Sure I cry. Whenever you do.

Sometimes, when it seems your wings have suddenly and unexpectedly been clipped, maybe, just maybe, there's more to learn by staying where you are.

Maybe not.

You decide.

It's one kind of victory
to slay a beast, move a mountain,
and cross a chasm. But it's another kind
altogether to realize that the beast and
the mountain and the chasm were
of your own design.

Well, by this point in the day,
if my calculations are correct, I expect
you've already begun thinking of yourself
as "mere mortal." Somewhat alone, a little bit
confused, and responsible for figuring out
how to make your life take off.

So . . . just thought I'd send you a reminder
that at this very moment, there are a million eyes
upon you, grateful for your courage; that you
already know all you need to know; and that
whether or not you can see it,
you're already soaring.

Bravo.

Do you know how
to give folks what they most, most,
most want from you without even asking
them what it is?

In all regards, just be yourself.

That's what they were after
when they manifested you into their lives.

Whoa!

*You are, truly,
one of a kind—and I would know.*

Funny . . . If you were to repeat
the following phrase every single hour
on the hour, or even just once every single day,
for months or years, what do you think
would eventually happen?

"I'm so sleepy, I'm just so tired,
it's all I can do to stay awake . . ."

I know, I know, you're way beyond this.
But here's a twist: What if, while bright-eyed
and wide-awake, feeling like you were in the best
shape of your life, brimming with vitality,
you began with the above mantra,
what would happen then?

Okay, okay, so you're an old soul. But what if
these things weren't said while in a deep,
meditative state, in an absolutely quiet room?
Would the results still be debilitating?

All right, Guru, I think I'm about to "get" you,
but first one more tease.

What if you didn't read another book on the
"nature of reality"? Didn't bother to hire a therapist?
Or follow a role model?

And you totally blew off the concepts of practicing, discipline, and sacrifice? Would your sleepy mantra still have any effect on you?

Oh my, I think I've done it! Have you ever before realized how ridiculously easy it is to transform your life? That no matter how poor you are today, or how deep in debt, or how bruised and tattered, or how unhealthy, or how lost, or how lonely . . . you already possess all the power, wisdom, and experience necessary to begin radically transforming your life by wisely choosing the words you speak, in spite of all evidence to the contrary?

Tallyho, abundant, triumphant, and happy soul.

Yeah, yeah, I know, I know you weren't born yesterday. And now you know that you "feel like a million bucks," that everything you "touch turns to gold," that you always "say the right thing at the right time," that "life is easy and fun," that your "path is clear," and that you "know exactly what to do" even if you can't yet "see" it.

Whatever you're going
to do today, please, do it to the best of
your ability. As if it was all that mattered;
as if it was all you had; and as if your very
happiness depended upon it. Because these
are among the very truths you came
here to learn.

It is understandably human nature
to see yourself as small.

Until you stop seeing yourself as just human.

Should be easy for you . . .

You are pure energy:
infinite, inexhaustible, and irresistible.

There are no challenges,
issues, or crises that do not contain
within them seeds of opportunity that could
not have otherwise existed.

Bet you didn't know how lucky you were!

It's wise not to ask others,
not even me, for much of anything—
guidance, help, time, comfort, security,
friendship, compassion, trust, respect, money,
love—that you yourself would not give.

Just a silly waste of time.

Give what you most want.

A Manifestation Tip
from your friend the Universe:

Feeling gratitude in advance,
before you even receive, as if you already had,
whether for direction or abundance
or anything else, opens the floodgates.

Did you catch the emphasis on feeling?

Ain't it grand?

You know, all the people, millions and millions and millions, who have gorgeous bodies that fill them with pride. Who've created enormous wealth—more than they could ever spend. Who have loving friends scattered all over the globe. And most have no more intelligence than a gopher.

They just didn't take "no" for an answer.

Think about it.

From a big-time gopher lover,
The Universe

Of course it's hard at first.
It's always hard at first. You're going
where you've never gone before in the
jungles of time and space. Cutting and hacking
and slicing your way through the thick,
clinging bush.

And though the scenery may seem like
it never changes, the day will come when,
from high on a new plateau, you'll look back
in total awe—amazed at the distance covered,
the perils faced, and the heights attained,

overcome by the inevitability of it all, bursting with pride, and struck most by the realization that the only true dangers you ever faced were during the times you felt like giving up or settling for less.

Yikes!
The Universe

And you're also gonna laugh like a hyena when you see that the tigers were made of paper and the lions were only me.

Have you heard my Tarzan impersonation? He taught me himself! I love, love, love impersonations. I do a great Jane, too. You'd never know it wasn't really her, believe me.

Actually, there isn't a soul on the planet that I haven't "done." And when I say "done," I mean "hang ten, all out, the Full Monty." Sometimes I get so carried away that I actually forget I'm the Universe! I hate when that happens. Quite the juxtaposition, if you can picture it. In one moment I'm the alpha and the omega, and everything in between. And in the next I'm yearning, pining, and dreaming poetically that one day, yes, one day, just maybe, if I work hard enough, if I'm good enough, if I'm not asking for too much, and if it's right for all concerned, my dreams will come true.

Can you imagine? Me?

You?

There are no finish lines in life,
yet perpetually seeking them, in terms of the
quick fix, the big win, or a home run, serves only
to remind you of what's missing, reinforcing the
imagined lack. However, when one stops looking
exclusively for results and embraces the journey
as it is, the days will soon be innumerable when,
looking back, you'll marvel at the distance covered.

Heigh-ho, Silver . . .

*It only seems to take a long time when
you're looking for finish lines, Kemosabi.*

In your wildest dreams,
did you ever expect it would seem so real?
That your pains and sorrows would cut so deep,
and that your joys and laughter would feel
so sublime?

No, I didn't think so, because one can't
know, until they go, which is why you're there.
To feel the emotions that can only be known
by immersing yourself in the illusions of have
and have not. Because in time and space, no
matter how much you have, there's always
more, and no matter how much you lack,

there's always less. Therefore, by simply being there, no matter what you do, or who you become, or how much you think you gain or lose, your purpose will be achieved.

To the winner's circle.

The slate is otherwise blank;
your thoughts, still, invariably
become the things and events of your life.
And just as much can be learned by
living in wealth and abundance as without . . .

So, let's do wealth and abundance.

It's like there are countless
rooms in the mansion of your mind. Some lavishly
appointed and others quite spartan. Rooms
bursting with their own creative energies that draw
you into action. And others that make you feel
frightened, angry, or resentful the moment you've
entered them. There are rooms that inspire
hope and foster new relationships. And others
filled with memories of what's already come
to pass and of dreams that never did.

It's like the more time you spend in any
given room, gazing from its windows,
the more the outside world begins to justify,
reinforce, and in every case, resemble it.

And it's like most people just think they find
themselves, at any given point in a day,
in one room or another without ever realizing
that every second of every day, they consciously
choose which room to hang out in.

Really, dear, it is your house . . .
But just a fig leaf?

Persistence,
persistence, persistence.

On the surface it might just seem like physical flailing, but spiritually, you're speaking directly to me and you're saying, "You hear me, and you hear me good! There ain't no way I'm doing without. I refuse to accept 'maybe,' 'sort of,' or 'not yet.' I am the power, the glory, and the way. My words quicken the ether, my actions fulfill their prophecy, and thy Kingdom come on earth, as it is in heaven . . . Pa-rum-pum-pum-pum."

And frankly, when confronted with such clarity . . . such style . . . such finesse, it makes my knees go wobbly and I'm like putty in your hands.

Rock on, rock on.

I just can't think of anything more
important to tell you than
"Congratulations, outstanding, well done!"

You are now, officially, the person
you once dreamed you'd become.

*Your courage and persistence have become
as legendary as your cooking.*

You know what's kind of wild?

At this very crossroads of time and space,
more than ever before, there are so many billions
of people yearning to awaken and understand the
truth about themselves, their divinity,
and the magic.

You know what else is kind of wild? Just as this
need arose, simultaneously, all over the world,
there have appeared the greatest teachers, though
in far smaller numbers, who have ever graced your
plane. Those who are actually living these truths,
leading with the example of their lives, and healing
those in need through simple conversation.

Want to know what's even more unbelievable?
That you sometimes consider
yourself more of the student.

*Nope, don't worry, it hasn't affected
your performance. You're already a legend.*

Actually, if you understood
the extraordinary gifts every single challenge
in your life makes possible, even inevitable,
you'd celebrate your challenges, new and old alike,
as the omens that they are of new beginnings,
spectacular change, and enhanced superpowers.

Perfect for where you are, huh?

*Any kind of "superpowers"
you can imagine . . .*

If I were a business professor
and you were my student, today's lesson
might sound like this:

Class . . . class . . . C-L-A-A-A-S-S!

In the "real" world, it's better to have loved
and lost, tried and failed, dreamed and missed,
than to sit out your turn in fear. Because the loss,
the failure, and the miss, however painful, are like
temporary market adjustments, soon forgotten.
Whereas the love, the adventure, and the dream
are like investments that, for the rest of your life
and beyond, never stop paying dividends.

Now, who brought me an apple?

Dr. Love

*Right you are! "How can you lose something
you're still capable of giving? How can you fail if
you haven't stopped trying? And how can you miss,
as long as your still aiming?" One Gold Star on
the forehead coming up, except . . . Someone
misspelled "you're" again.*

Oh, what a shame.

It's not the size of your dreams
that determines whether or not they come true,
but the size of the actions you take that implies
their inevitable arrival.

Your greatest admirer,
The Universe

*And just so you know . . . the bigger the dream,
the bigger the action.*

Whoohoooooo! Great news!

Everything, absolutely everything you've ever wanted, now lies within reach!

Of course . . . you still have to reach.

Hey, you have to admit,
that's a pretty small price for "everything."

Hup! Stop! No! No! No!

Thinking about "how," weren't you? How you're going to get from "here to there" kind of thoughts. The cursed hows. Bummer, huh?

There's nothing quite as demoralizing in the human experience as trying to use your brain to map the unseen, because immediately you sense it's hopeless . . . and you're right!

You can't map the unseen! But I can.

You just need to define "there" and get busy doing what you can in every direction that feels right, though insisting upon none.

Do the logical things (like knocking on doors and turning over stones). Do the spiritual things (like visualizing and taking catnaps). And leave the accidents, coincidences, and spontaneous illumination to me.

In a way, it's almost like throwing paint on the wall, and then trusting me to connect the dots. Because I will, and the resulting masterpiece will blow you away.
I promise.

After all, who do you think gave the Mona Lisa *her smile?*

71

Dreams are like that . . .

Most of the time you don't even know how close
you are, until after they've come true.

Sometimes, even, the very day before they come
true, it still feels like they're a million miles away.

Something to remember.

*I think it works like this because if you knew
how close you really were, you'd probably get
so nervous that your legs would shake, your voice
would break, and you'd come so undone that
we'd have to call for a "do-over."*

The easiest way
to avoid letdowns and disappointments, is . . .

No, it's not lowering your standards.
That's quitting.

No, it's not releasing expectations.
That's an old wives' tale.

And no, it's not relinquishing all mortal desires.
That's an Oriental religion.

It's never tricking yourself into thinking
that your happiness is dependant upon the
things and events of time and space, or
what other people think, say, and do.

*And no, it's never really had anything to do
with chocolate. That was the Cookie Monster.*

Just because all things
are possible, doesn't mean you're supposed
to do all things.

*Besides, it's not as if you aren't
going to live forever.*

Do it your way
and you'll win the attention,
and the respect, of the whole world.

Not that you need it.

Ever wonder how much patience
you should have with someone
before you lose your temper?

Infinite.

But careful, now. That doesn't mean you
have to wait for them, stay with them, or hang
around them. Lord, no. It just means that for
as long as you choose to keep them in your life,
understanding them, not changing them,
is everything.

You couldn't be freer.

Isn't it strange
how you can find metaphors for life
absolutely everywhere?

I mean, here I sit at the coffee shop
and everything seems to be a parody
of time and space.

The smiles and warmth that greet you
around every corner mirror your own.

After you place your order and
do what you know to do, you expectantly
trust you'll be served.

Worrying about the hows is ludicrous.

And over at the sidebar,
the really sweet stuff . . . is free.

Whoops . . . there . . . right there . . . lower . . .
You've got some foam on the tip of your nose.
And yes, we have coffee here. We have everything
here (first, I might add).

Believe me, I know all about it.
I know the stress. I know the frustration.
I know the temptations of time and space.
We worked this out ahead of time.
They're part of the plan. We knew this stuff
might happen. Actually, you insisted they
be triggered whenever you were ready
to begin thinking thoughts you've never
thought before.

Good on you.

A Community Service Reminder
from the Universe.

YOU RULE.

Your gifts are innumerable.

Your insights are profound.

Your choices are endless.

Your touch is healing.

Your thoughts become things.

Your power is indescribable.

And you are loved and adored,
on a moment-to-moment basis more
than you can now understand.

YOU RULE.

Do you know

what it's going to feel like when the day comes and everything you now want has come to pass? When you're living in total abundance, in perfect health, looking fabulous, with friends and laughter wherever you go?

It's going to feel like, "Yeah . . . of course."

That's how well I know you.

Sometimes, not always,
but sometimes, being logical doesn't negate
the magic, it stirs it up, because not all
miracles hide in the unseen.

Don't be afraid to do the obvious . . .
really well.

*Sometimes miracles even hang around,
waiting for you to call, write, or show up.*

It's as if when you move, I move.
When you reach, I reach. And when you
go the extra mile, I clear the way . . .
but not one single moment sooner.

Which is why, before you commit,
things can sometimes look pretty scary.

"Just like that."

A heartfelt compliment
given for no other reason than
because it's meant, is never, ever forgotten.

You've got the power.

*And that's not just because I move in the lips
that speak them, but also in the ears that hear.*

When the choice is to hurt
or be hurt. Cheat or be cheated.
Violate or be violated.

Always, always,
always choose the latter.

Trust me.

*Besides, predicaments like these
don't just happen.*

This might sound a bit conceited,
but there's a part of me that's human, too
(if you know what I mean).

I'm a big-picture person, and from here
I can see all of you. ALL that you've been through,
every decision you've ever made, and I know exactly
where you're headed. I know your every hope,
dream, and fear. I've seen you at your "best"
and your "worst," on good days and bad.
And I gotta confess, I couldn't possibly be
prouder of who I've become.

Yeah, me.

So I was thinking . . .

I know you know that there's the "you"
that you know you are—adventurous,
good-looking, and fun to be around.

And I know you know that there's another
part of "you" in the unseen who you've kind of
temporarily forgotten—who completes you,
loves you, and knows what's really going on.

Well, how'd you like it if I removed the veils?
Just for a second? Gave you a glimpse of who
that special, divine, otherworldly essence is,
so that you might at last begin to comprehend
how extraordinary, sublime, and
divine you really are?

Okay . . . It's me.
The entire Universe.

Surprise, surprise, surprise.

What?
You were expecting some little Tinker Bell?

It's not a matter of feeling
worthy of love, friends, health, or wealth.
Or of appreciating what you already have.
Or even of learning to love yourself. These don't
have to come first. You don't have to wear a
halo to manifest the changes you want.

It's simply a matter of understanding that if
you do your part, visualize, prepare the way,
and act "as if" without looking back over your
shoulder for quick results, what you want *must*
be added unto you, as will the feelings
of worthiness, appreciation, and loving your
hot-bodied self.

You're prequalified to rock the world.
There are no other rules.

Besides, feeling unworthy does not make you so.

Anger is one of enlightenment's
many barometers.

Basically, the more you have of one,
the less you have of the other.

Yessiree, Bob.

Don't get mad, get smart.

Do you know

what's already happened this month?
A million Beethovens were born.
A million Picassos.
A million Einsteins.
A million Florence Nightingales.
A million Martin Luther Kings.
And a million Madame Curies,
to name just a few. Each as capable of
moving mountains, touching lives,
and leaving the world far better
than they found it.

And so you can just imagine how all of us
"here" watch in anticipation to see which
ones will have the courage to do whatever
little they can each day, with what little
they've got, from where they are,
before their baby steps turn into
giant leaps for all.

It's so in you.

Not desire, but expectation,
unlocks wheels, parts seas, moves mountains,
and changes everything.

To put this tactfully . . .
If you don't start doing stuff to prepare
for all the fun changes that are about to
take place in your life, j-e-e-e-z,
I just don't know what might happen.

But I'm darn sure I know what won't.

I'm not from the IRS, but I'm here to help.

I'm also crazy about you!

If ever there was a symbiotic
relationship, you know, like leaf hoppers
and meat ants, clownfish and ritteri sea
anemones, the Egyptian plover bird and
the crocodile, each of which thrives because
of the existence of the other,
it's me and you, babe.

Include me in your every thought,
as I do you.

You have something in your teeth.

Of course, I think unceasingly of you.
You threatened to eat me alive if I ever forgot.

Holy Hannah!

I just realized how few people there are
in the world like you. Who have your sense
of compassion. Your penetrating insights.
And your extraordinary zest for life.

What was I thinking about?

Oh yeah, my image.

We rock.

*Thought it was too much to be coincidence.
And while all the rest are in my image, too,
somehow not a single one has quite your style
and "savoir faire."*

Hmm . . .

In the time that it takes you
to read this short Note, you could have planted
a new image in your mind (anything you like,
ideally with an emotional charge), I could have
reacted (realigning planets, people, and the sort),
and the floodgates would've begun trembling
violently as we'd have been drawn infinitely
closer to manifesting the vision you'd chosen.

Fortunately, there's still time.

It doesn't have to be hard or take a lot of time.
Visualize, it's the least you can do.

One hundred years from now,
it will not matter what was in your bank
account, what kind of car you drove,
or what style of home you lived in.

On the other hand, since one of the reasons
you're in time and space is to understand
that you do, indeed, have dominion over
all things . . . nailing these early on
would be way cool.

*And what better way to be important
in the eyes of a child than to live your power
so that they might observe and learn to live theirs?*

In all tests of character,
when two viewpoints are pitted against each other,
in the final analysis, the thing that will strike you
the most is not who was right or wrong, strong
or weak, wise or foolish . . . but who went to the
greater length in considering the
other's perspective.

Don't you agree?

*Well, yeah, I did mean the final, final analysis,
but you'll see, that one really counts big.*

If you know what you want,
if you've made up your mind, if you can see it,
feel it, and move toward it in some small way
every single day . . . it has to happen.

Changing one's life is easy

and there are lots of ways to go about it,
though all exact some sort of price:

Pinpointing invisible, limiting, self-sabotaging
beliefs—extremely demanding on brain cells
and much easier to do if you have a friend who
channels the dead, but either way, it'll keep you
busy for the rest of your life.

Discovering what occurrences in the past
have misprogrammed you—a therapist can help,
though expensive if you don't have insurance,
but you can both pretend you're a complex
person and that if it wasn't for your childhood,
you'd have the perfect life.

Distinguishing between those who really love
you and those who just wish to use you—

super tricky, and may destroy perfectly good relationships, but with a good lawyer you can laugh all the way to the bank while accepting little or no responsibility for your own happiness.

These are just a few of the most popular and widely written-about methods. Of course, you could also just begin imagining and moving toward the life of your dreams, treating everyone with kindness, and assuming all is well— profoundly and radically effective for both short- and long-term gains, but totally lacking in drama, requires solo efforts, and is much too easy for most people to take seriously.

Oh well,
The Universe

Talking a lot about something
that bothers you is a pretty good sign
that you've got something huge and
profoundly liberating to learn.

Whooohooooo!

*That is, if you can catch yourself,
turn within, and yearn for illumination.*

To err on the side of generosity,
patience, and kindness . . . is not to err.
Because no little thing slips by me
that isn't returned bigger and better.

Hey! I've been looking
over all my old photos, and yes,
you guessed it, you look absolutely smashing.
But honestly, if you don't mind my saying so,
you're never quite as beautiful in a photograph—
mine or anyone else's—as you are in person.
Not even close.

The odd quiver of your lip, the sparkle
in your eye, and the hidden question mark,
sometimes, when you smile. The confidence
behind your laughter, the concern behind
your tears, and the unpredictability of your wit.

The reassurance of your glance,
the easiness of your presence, and the
"junk in your trunk." I wouldn't change
one single thing. But you guessed that,
too, huh?

Isn't it strange, though, how some still
expect to see all that when looking at a
photo of themselves, or just staring,
motionless, into a mirror?

Maybe if they at least waved?

If anyone should ever ask
if you're enlightened . . .

ALWAYS SAY YES!

Same goes for being healthy, wealthy,
and loved beyond imagination.

Got it?

The Universe

Your word is your wand.

Wow! What an incredible year!

Lots of "firsts," tons of breakthroughs, countless miracles. Stones overturned, doors unlocked, and journeys just begun. It feels like I've waited an eternity for all that's now happening. (Actually, I have.)

Do you have any idea how many millenniums, billenniums, trillenniums have gone by without you in the world? Thinking the kind of thoughts you now think, doing the kind of stuff you now do, and illuminating all the nooks and crannies (n-o-o-o-o, I didn't almost say "crooks and grannies") of the planet I couldn't otherwise reach?

Too many.

Thanks, and have a great day!

Your fellow Adventurer,
The Universe

*Well worth the wait.
But next time I create a reality, would you mind, terribly, being among the first to visit?*

Whoops . . .

ever since I began handing out wings and
giving dominion to those made in my image,
there seems to be the misconception that happiness
will come from doing, being, and having it all
when actually, as you well know,
it's the other way around.

You want to tell 'em?

And, yes. You do have wings.

You know,
it seems a shame that for many,
life doesn't seem fair.

But perhaps that's one of the reasons you
were summoned: to make life a little more
bearable for them until they learn how fair it is,
and so that they can then do the same for others.

So . . .
Did they get a good deal, or what?

And when I say "perhaps,"
it's just diplomacy.

The slate's been wiped clean,

the past has released its grip, and before you sparkles
eternity yearning for direction. All that now stands
between you and the life of your dreams is just one
teeny, tiny, gentle, little rule. Only one condition,
prerequisite, principle that matters.

It's not love. It's not God. It's not fate, or luck, or
karma. It's not complicated or esoteric, and you
needn't sacrifice, plead, or pray to invoke it. It's the
only rule that's ever existed, and it's the only one
that ever will exist. No reality can exist in its absence.
For its mere existence, you are. With its existence,
the power, the light, and the way are revealed. It's
your purpose to discover it, and it's your destiny
to master it. It's the beginning, the middle, and
the end. The alpha and the omega. The be-all
and end-all of every wish, desire, and dream,
and you are its keeper.

This caveat of all caveats is that absolutely nothing
can be anything until it is first imagined. Thoughts
become things, nothing else does. And so, it's the
thoughts you choose from here on out that will
become the things and events of your life,

forevermore. It is written in stone. There's no other way. It's your ticket to anywhere you can dream of. Your passport to abundance, health, and friendships. The key to the palace of your wildest dreams.

Your thoughts, and your thoughts alone, will set you in motion. Your thoughts will yield the inspiration, creativity, and determination you need. Your thoughts will orchestrate the magic and inspire the Universe. Your thoughts will carry you to the finish line if you just keep thinking them. Never give up. Never waver, doubt, or ask.

Aim high.

That you've even received this Note, that you're able to read it through, means you are so close. So extraordinarily close. The hardest work has been done. The wars have already been waged. The lessons have already been learned. The journey, now, is for home.

You're so deserving. You're ready.
It's all that stands between you and
the life of your dreams.

What's worse than being human
and hearing fingernails scrape a chalkboard?

Being the Universe and hearing
"May I? Can I? Will I?" instead of
"Thank you. Thank you. Thank you."

Makes my face squinch up.

I'd even prefer
"Hubba. Hubba. Hubba."

Let's see, last time I checked
you were still a forever being with as many
second chances and new romances saved up
as there are stars in the night sky; whose thoughts
fly on wings, whose dreams become things, and
for whom all the elements bow. (Just in case
you were wondering.)

*Where is it? Where is it?! Have you seen
your future lately . . . ? Oh, there it is! Spinning
in the palm of your hand.*

Best I can figure,
the reason some get down-and-out,
lose motivation, and watch too much TV
is that they've somehow forgotten just how fast
things can change, and they've yet to discover
just how good they can get.

Even you are going to be surprised.

Not that I don't check in on Howard Stern
every now and then, myself.

Remember when it was really fun
to catch raindrops on your tongue, walk under
archways because they were there, and roll around
in the sand at the beach? To go all the way to the
store for a tiny treat, lie on the grass looking
for "God" in the clouds, and make scary monster
faces in the mirror? To watch the stars because
they were winking at you, count the flowers in
the garden by the door, and put Cocoa Puffs
up your nose?

Well, I'm happy to inform you,
most of it still is.

Ah-h-h-h-h-h-h-h . . .

Whoohoooo, you're alive!

Much is said about the lust
for material things, so if I may add to the
chorus . . . Go for it!

After all, matter is pure spirit,
only more so.

You know how
when you visualize something every day,
to such a degree that you can literally taste
its reality? And you believe in the likelihood
of its manifestation with all your heart and soul?
And as often as you think of it, in at least some
small way, you prepare for its arrival? Yet still
absolutely nothing happens?

Right! That's impossible.

*Just do your part, I'll do mine,
and everything has to change.*

Aha!
Do you know what your
thoughts did last week?!

Oh, yes you do.

They became the things and events of this week.
The things you thought would be difficult became
difficult; easy became easy; boring became boring;
and fun became fun. Where you thought there
might be surprises, you were surprised. And
where you thought there might be land mines,
there were land mines.

Bravo! You can add last week to the list of
your most creative accomplishments.

Now, can you guess what your thoughts
this week are going to do?

*Please, choose every single one of them
as if nothing else mattered.*

Things only get better.

Yeah, I know,
not everyone will be ready for that one . . .
But they're getting better.

Brace yourself!
It's time for more "good news, bad news."

The good news is that life is just an illusion.
A playground of sorts for spiritual adventurers
to learn of their divinity. Where absolutely
anything can happen, thoughts become things,
and dreams do come true. It's like the ultimate
test pilot's paradise, where they can crash and burn,
and do it again. Soar and learn. Rise and fall.
Conquer and stall. Or just fly in circles, sometimes
on purpose, sometimes not. All while lifting the
entire Universe—every imaginable form of

consciousness—higher into the light for their tears-and-laughter-bought lessons.

The bad news?

You're the test pilot.

Our hero and ace,
The Universe

Ha, "bad news."
You're an unlimited being of light;
loved and adored; without beginning or end;
invincible, unlimited, almighty . . .
Bad news? I don't think so.

It goes like this . . .
Whatever you're capable of summoning,
imagining, and moving toward, however feebly
to begin with, I am capable of delivering.

In expectation,
The Universe

Careful, now, 'cause you are gonna get it!

You need never doubt
that I tirelessly conspire on your behalf.
Because if it hasn't occurred to you yet,
I need you as much as you need me.
To show me the way, to give me each day,
and to go where I couldn't otherwise go.

Amen,
The Universe

You complete me.

No matter what else
you might feel or think, it's working, flawlessly,
magically, and without exception. Your thoughts,
beliefs, and expectations are the sole cause of
the effects of your life. And while this may give
you pause and have you wondering why you've not
yet met with some of the successes you've sought,
let it also empower you as you remember that the
floodgates must fly open and the Kingdom must be
revealed at the precise moment when you release
whatever else you might have felt or thought
about it not working.

There are some folks
who think that life isn't fair,
and to them I say, "Touché!"

Obviously, they see themselves as unlimited
Beings of Light for whom all things are possible.
They recognize that their thoughts become things,
giving rise not only to dreams, but to worlds. And
they appreciate that their very existence in time
and space proves that they're loved
beyond imagination.

Yes, these are the folks who understand that
with dominion over all things, the cards of life
are indeed stacked in their favor.

N'est-ce pas?
You couldn't be more favored.

It's never, never, never
too late to give thanks in advance for the help
you stand in need of, as if you've already received it.
Because you just wouldn't believe how much I can
accomplish in no time at all, literally.

Thanks for listening.

See? It works.

Scary? You bet it's scary!

Package yourself up into a little ball of energy. Deliberately forget that you're everywhere, always, at once—the sun, the moon, and the stars. Expose yourself, as a tiny baby, no less, to the minds of those who are as lost as you—however well-meaning. Adopt their beliefs. Play their games. Spend much of your life living by their rules. And trust that you just happen to notice that your thoughts still, invariably, without exception, become the things and events of your life. Have faith that you're open-minded enough to accept that you're the cause, if you believe in effects; accept responsibility for everything that has, or has not, ever happened to you. So that, finally, you recognize your unmitigated superpowers, claim them, and rock the world!

I'm terrified. It may well be my finest work. How do I follow up on creating a reality like that?

Yes, we'll think of something adventurous.

Lots of people wonder . . .
Fewer take the time to really think . . .

But I'll be darned; sometimes I think I could count on the fingers of my hand how many actually visualize the life of their dreams, as if their dreams had already come true, every single day, for just five minutes or so.

Do it till you're satisfied.

Yeah, big hands, lots of fingers, but still.

How totally cool!
Last night we were dreaming together!

Do you remember? Soaring in and out of mile-high clouds. Walking upon lazy lakes and raging rivers. Manifesting gold coins from our blue-jean pockets. Reaching out to the many who are only just now discovering that thriving is their natural state, that abundance is their birthright, and that friends, guides, and admirers are only ever a nod away.

Shoot. You were right.
You said you wouldn't remember a thing.

Well, that's okay. I was right, too.
I said that those you helped would never forget.
Just like here.

See you tonight,
The Universe

Ain't immortality grand?

Is it just me,
or does it all seem far too good
to possibly be true?

*And among other things,
how many different flavors of chocolate
does one really need?*

There's always a way.
Though chances are, it's not the one
that first comes to mind.

*Commit only to the end result,
drop the "cursed hows," and be unfettered
by closed doors, dashed hopes,
and broken promises.*

Your balance of
wit, charm, and intelligence . . .

The measures of your endurance,
strength, and stamina . . .

The depths of your sensitivity,
passion, and leanings . . .

It's never, not ever, been done before.

Now, do you think these things were all
proportioned accidentally? Or do you think
they were my idea, designed to take me
where others couldn't go?

Bingo.

*Well, yeah, kind of like that neat Mars Rover,
but on Earth, without the "bugs," and cuter.*

The thing about success
is that she often arrives at such a late hour that
only the oddballs, freaks, and nuts (you know,
the ones who continued believing, in spite of
all worldly evidence to the contrary)
remain to greet her.

A little weird is good.

The Universe

*Well, she doesn't have to arrive so late,
but sometimes that's also how long it takes
before people stop fretting about whether
or not she ever will.*

It's not the dazzling voice
that makes a singer. Or clever stories that make
a writer. And it's not piles of money that
make a tycoon.

It's having a dream and wanting to live it
so greatly that one would rather move with it
and "fail" than succeed in another realm.

You so have what it takes.

*At which point, of course, failure becomes impossible,
joy becomes the measure of success, and fitting into
the jeans you wore back-in-the-day, inevitable.
Hubba, hubba.*

Do you have any idea
how thoroughly, utterly, and completely
I want the very things you now want?

Well, let's just say that after visualizing,
and expecting, and acting with faith,
then came you.

We're in this together.

Banzai—
The Universe

May you live ten thousand years!
(As if you haven't already.)

Ye-e-e-h-a-a-a-w! FRIDAY!
Do you know what that means?

It means you've still got time.
It means it's still your turn.
It means I can't stop loving you.

XOXO,
The Universe

Ye-e-e-h-a-a-a-w! MONDAY!
Do you know what that means?

It means you're dreaming. In a place where your
thoughts become the things and events of
your life. And in this dream you're about to
manifest, yet again, a brand-new adventure
framed by the illusion of seven days. And any
villains or heroes you encounter this week;
any highs or lows; strikeouts, base hits, or
home runs; Mack Daddies, Sugar Babies,
or Oprah Winfreys . . . will be of
your own design.

*Ah! If you "do" an Oprah,
please tell her about these Notes!*

Ye-e-e-h-a-a-a-w! TUESDAY!
Just kidding.

Ahem . . .
Even though this will seem like a lie:

No one can be lied to who has not first,
somehow, someway, lied to themselves.

Self-deception is really the only kind there is.

There's nothing wrong
with wanting "more."

It means you're alive and well.

*Actually,
you're "supposed" to want more.*

Have you heard the one about the little boy who asked his mom why people don't fly? She told him, "It's mostly because they forget they have wings."

Sorry, not really funny, but I just didn't want you to forget about yours.

To the stars,
The Universe

If it wasn't for needing you
there so much, I'd need you here.

"Thanks," on behalf of all those in your life
right now who are just too busy, or stressed,
or sad to see how much you add to theirs.
(You know who I mean.)

The Universe

I'm not wild about cloning,
unless they're talking about you.

Rule #1 for Giving:

Expect not that your Kingdom will come,
or your bounty will be multiplied,
via the recipient of your kindness.

Drives me absolutely, totally crazy—
and severely limits my options.

Besides, I've always preferred surprising you.

If you only knew how many
miracles you've already performed,
nothing would ever again overwhelm you,
frighten you, or seem impossible.

And you'd begin admiring yourself,
as we always have.

Just a word from you,
just a word—and I'm there.

No matter where "there" is. No matter what
you want. No matter what you need. No matter
where you've been. No matter where you're headed.
No matter when you ask. No matter how you ask.
No matter who's there with you. No matter who
else you're thinking of. No matter what,
no matter what, no matter what.

Please, believe me,
The Universe

And I travel with all the angels—
every single one of them—
with just a word from you.

Of course dreams come true.
Just look around you. Out the window.
Down the hall. Into the mirror. These were
all once dreams of mine.

And I had a whole lot less to work with.

As you've probably deduced
by now, I don't think in terms of reasonable
or unreasonable, likely or unlikely, possible or
impossible. I merely figure out the "hows."

Guess what that leaves you with?

Let's give them something to talk about.

You have a track record here,
have you forgotten?

Little . . . teensy . . . tiny . . .
That's how all of your present issues, challenges,
and so-called problems will one day soon appear.

And then you'll wonder—one hot summer's eve
as you're floating lazily across your swimming pool
(hidden orchestra playing loudly in the background),
healthy, confident, and just beaming about your
recent successes in real estate; toned, sculpted,
and tanned, carelessly splashing your friends,
telling jokes, and occasionally laughing so hard
you almost capsize—how you could've ever
thought they were such a big deal.

I know you.

You call that thing a bathing suit?

If you were to ask me,
I'd probably say that the number one cause
of loneliness in time and space is not a lack of
friends, but a lack of keeping busy.

I'd even go so far as to say that nine out of ten
times the solution to every crisis, challenge,
or problem—in relationships, careers, or
otherwise—is to get busy.

Because when you get busy, you allow me to
slide whatever you most need—be it material,
spiritual, or a new friend; answers, ideas, or
comfort—right under your big ol' nose.

The one time out of ten?
It's to first be still—and then get busy.

Beneath your luminous skin,
just behind the sparkle of your eyes,
emanating from the depths of your soul,
there's a fire-breathing dragon, possessing
unimaginable strength, wisdom, and
thoughts that reach out and sizzle
every corner of the Universe.

A playful dragon. A fearless dragon.
A good-looking dragon. Colossal, yet swift;
spontaneous, yet clever; unreasonable,
yet measured; outrageous, yet innocent;
determined, yet patient; cautious, yet carefree;
light, yet less filling.

A predator, guardian,
and connoisseur of adventure.

And I think it's really cool how, lately,
I'm seeing more and more of it come out.

Gives new meaning to "hottie."

Bagnnn . . . Bagnnnn . . . Bagnnnn . . .
We interrupt your day with a test,
a test of the Emergency Broadcast System.

Can you see me, right now?

Yes—I'm the light, and all it shines on.

Can you hear me?

Yep—every single sound,
and the silence, too.

Can you feel me? Right now? In the air on your
skin, under your feet, and in the palms of your
hands? The tug at your heart, the rhythm it
keeps, and the blood in your veins?

Right. Now, next time you have cause for alarm,
see me. Next time you need absolutely anything,
listen to me. And next time you feel all alone,
remember you're not.

Once you make up your mind
and start something, commit to it, say "Yes!,"
and never look back. Do you have any doubt,
any whatsoever, that I will not rush to your side?

That legions won't be summoned? That players
won't be drawn to your corner? Connections made?
Circumstances crafted? Dots connected?

That the course of history
won't be irrevocably changed?

Good, I didn't think so.

I'd say you're ready.

Was that a "Yes!"?

Oh, shoot!

Did I remember to ask you to turn off the lights?
You know, in the "Hall of Records" after I showed
you where all the books written about you were?

Remember, not a word to anyone!
(Most don't believe in traversing time, yet,
and they'll think you're whacked.)

S-h-h-h-h . . .

The Universe

*Told you. You put on quite a show, didn't you?
Changed the bloomin' world.*

Persistence is priceless,
but its value lies in doing, doing, doing, not in
waiting, waiting, waiting.

Okay? Okay? Okay?

The Universe

*Not that you were hanging around for someone,
someway, or somehow!*

It totally flips me out.
People talk to me, they ask me stuff,
they show me things, yet so rarely do they
ever expect a reply.

Am I invisible or something?

Well, enlightenment
is kind of like flying for
the first time without wings.

Of course, there's the exhilaration,
the happiness, and the intoxicating sense
of freedom that's almost indescribable.

But there's also the subtle shock at what you
now see as the inevitability of your accomplishment.
The wonderment of how you hadn't seen this so
clearly before, mingled with acceptance. And the
dim recognition that it's part of some distant
agreement you once made.

And, at last, as you come to your senses and finally
think to gaze below, upon the tiny jewel you've
called home for so long, you're struck with a jolt
as you see it so magically and effortlessly
suspended—floating—in space, and you realize,
for the first time, that even there you were
flying all along.

Up ahead!!!
There's a tree coming right at you!

You know those feelings of
euphoria, excitement, and inspiration that send your
spirit soaring?

Well, they're just me and all the angels, finally
rushing through one of the many doors you've
knocked upon, down the hall, and dancing into the
light of your searching heart.

And those feelings of depression, sadness,
and powerlessness that make you feel like you're
carrying the weight of the world on your shoulders?

They're us, too. Reminding you that there are
still a few more doors to try.

Let's get this party started.

When it comes to "having it all,"
many fine, young souls take issue with the word
"have." They're concerned about the concept
of ownership. Their soul is taunted by a guilt for
the pleasure it derives from material things.
And they quiver at the thought of "others"
having less than they have.

Of course, such righteous and selfless thoughts
are a significant contributor to the creation
of lack in a world of endless abundance,
but they'll learn.

"Kids . . . !"

Whoohoo!

The script for the most amazing time in your life is nearing perfection! We're so excited and happy for you. Bravo. Bravo. Bravo.

It's complete with friends and laughter, wealth and abundance, health and harmony. And best of all, there are going to be some really neat surprises. BIG surprises! Really HUGE, Texas style.

And you're gonna say,
"B-bu . . . but . . . I . . . I . . . I . . .
H-Ho . . . How? Never in all my life
have I imagined such outrageousness! All my expectations have been exceeded! Never have I dreamed of being so blessed!" And we're gonna say, "Oh, yes you did."

And you're gonna say, "Oh, no I didn't."

And we'll say, "Did."

And you'll say, "Didn't."

And then we'll remind you of those occasions when you simply saw yourself happy. Visualizing euphoric happiness, bypassing the details. Smiling from ear to ear in your mind's eye, pumping your fist, dialing your friends' cell-phone numbers with shaking fingers, happy tears running down your face, when you left all of the "hows" to the Universe.

And you're gonna say, "Oh."

And we're gonna say, through tears of our own, "Nice hows, huh?"

"Action!"

Have you ever thought of writing for the movies?

157

Actually, if it were any easier,
it wouldn't be worth it.

You'll see.

Do you think having your own
private little planet where you could have,
do, and be anything you dreamed of, with as many
friends as you choose, would be worth it,
if the price of admission was to forget
how you got there so that you could discover
your throne, on your own?

All bow.

You always were a trendsetter.
But do you have any idea how many others
I've had to strike the same bargain with?

One more thought on the "hows."

Just because you're not to mess with them doesn't mean you're not to get busy doing all you can, with what you've got, from where you are.

The difference is in how you see what you do: you don't do all you can with an eye to hitting a home run, but with an understanding that for each door you knock upon and every stone you turn over, you're pitching the ball to me.

The more balls you pitch, the greater my options, and the farther the balls will sail.

Batter up,
The Universe

*It's like, if you want me to do ALL I can
(move mountains and that sort of thing),
you must do ALL you can
(cast-your-bread sort of thing).*

How to make anything happen . . .
Act as if it already has, and never look back.

Thanks for being there,
even through the "hard" times.

And sorry if they've ever seemed like too much.
But I'm pretty sure it was you, after all,
who said, "I want it all—no matter the cost."

You power shopper, you.

The Universe

For just a moment,
can you imagine that on the day the earth
was created, I'd want to experience her in
every imaginable form?

Good.

Now can you imagine that when it came
to creating the animals, I couldn't just pick one—
but would want to soar through the skies, swim
in the oceans, and burrow in the fields?

Excellent. I had to be all of her animals,
to experience all of their secrets.

So when it came to having dominion over
all things, it must now be just as obvious
that I had to be everyone.

And I am.

I walk in your shoes. Every day.

Do you remember
way back when, on the day you first earned
your wings, how you worried about whether
or not you'd be able to use them to lift yourself,
and thereby the entire planet, higher?

And so I reminded you that the reason
you earned them was because you already had?

You've already earned all that your heart desires.

*Besides, you didn't really think with all the encrusted
diamonds, inlaid pearls, and the monogrammed gold
flaps you special-ordered, they were really about flying
even higher, did you? I don't even know how you walk
around with them things. But I'm proud as can be.*

Of course it's true
everyone's born with a gift. One that will allow
them to fill a special place in the Universe that
absolutely no one else can fill. A blessing that
makes all other blessings pale in comparison.
A gift of incalculable value to the entire world
when it's uncovered, explored, and embraced.

Yours?

Being you.

*WOW, you must have known someone
really "high up"!*

Universal Personality Test:

Want to know how to tell whether you were born with the gift to heal? Or perhaps if your strengths lie in leadership? If you're a left- or right-"brained" individual? Whether or not you're truly a "people person"? Whether or not, given your beliefs . . . friends, laughter, and abundance will flow to you effortlessly, or should be diligently sought after?

Just decide.

It's always worked before.

The adulation. The worship.
The glory. The throngs. The masses. The fans.

You'd think by now the novelty would have
worn off—but those few (and I do mean few,
by our standards) who are brave enough to
adventure into the jungles of time and space
have our deepest admiration.

Because even though we know that wherever
they find themselves, nothing will be as it seems;
that no matter what happens, they'll always be
safe and protected; and that their inevitable
homecoming celebration will make the Academy
Awards look like a McDonald's Happy Meal,
they know none of this. And so the heights of
their glory and the depths of their despair
have become legend in a land of legends.

*And you thought "reality TV" was popular?
You should see your ratings!*

I'm hungry!
Hungry for adventure.

The adventure of love.

Tell you what:
The more of it you give today
to the least deserving on your list,
the more your life will change.

Oh, they love me all right!
They really, really love me.

But sometimes I wonder if the reason
they love me has anything to do with the thought
that one day, just maybe, I'm going to be the spark,
ignite the fire, and summon the magic that will
make all of their dreams come true.

*Yikes, are they ever going to be surprised
when they find out that's their job?*

Have you heard about the
"Bewitching Hour"?

Actually, it's top secret, so I'll whisper.

Every single morning, ever since time began, before the sun even rises, the drums start beating, the choirs start singing, the energy starts rising, and every single soul who has ever lived scurries around the plane of manifestation as a chanting begins . . . And gets louder and louder . . . And goes faster and faster until . . . a feverish pitch is reached and the celestial skies part with a clap of thunder, revealing billions upon billions of the most beautiful angels you have ever seen. Flying down from the heavens, some with wings outstretched, others with wings pointed back. Darting, diving, banking, and rolling—some so fast they're only a blur—while others seem to float by as if catching what remained of a midsummer night's breeze.

Every one of them a reflection of the greatest, the loveliest, and the highest I've ever imagined. Every one of them a messenger of hope, and peace, and joy; healers and teachers, comforters and creators. And every one of them about to greet a brand-new day in time and space with a morning yawn, sleepy eyes, and the power to
ROCK THE WORLD.

This is the "Bewitching Hour." Shhhh . . .

And if you listen real hard,
you can still hear the drums.

Hosanna in the highest.

*Nice inverted-triple-axel-gallactica this morning.
Seems like just yesterday when you were still
somersaulting the whole way—doesn't it?*

Oh, hi . . .

at least you are still talking to me.
Was just sitting here on the beach wondering
whether or not the whole thing was a good idea
in the first place, you know?

When the idea first dawned on me, it just seemed
like one heck of an adventure. Endless possibilities.
Incomparable camaraderie. A little bit of me in
everyone (okay, a lot). My style, my rhythm, my
appetite for fun.

I had no idea people could feel so lost . . .
So sad. So alone.

Well, this much I know for sure: next time I throw a
"bring your out-of-body" party in the middle of the
night, we won't turn off the music at the sound of the
first alarm clock. Escorts will be provided upon reentry
to avoid accidental body swapping. And illumination,
guardianship, and inspiration shall be made available
at all times for those who are confused, just like on
earth, as long as they ask and expect to be heard.
Shake your tail feathas . . .

The Universe

What did you think I was talking about?
By the way, loved your kilt. Where it fit.

If you ever find yourself driving down the motorway of life looking for an exit that says EASY STREET, may I remind you that that's where you got on, following a sign that said PARADISE, THIS WAY. ROAD UNDER CONSTRUCTION. WATCH OUT FOR "LIGHT WORKERS," FALLING DEBRIS, POTHOLES, AND SLIPPERY PATCHES. NO TURNING BACK.

And you said, "Cool."

What do you mean, "Are we there yet?" You're now one of the light workers.

Rising suns and babbling brooks.

Tropical forests and sleeping meadows.

Modern marvels and scientific breakthroughs.

Exciting discoveries and limitless frontiers.

Devoted friends and caring strangers.

Lives and loves and souls to hold
so close, one's own heart could burst.

Look at it like this: it's not so much that you
have to wait for your dreams to come true,
but that you *get to*—in a Garden of Eden,
the paradise of paradises, in the palm
of my hand.

Can you even count the splendors?

Here's a little "Inevitability Test"
to check on the progress you're making toward
achieving any particular dream.

You're pretty much doing something about it,
every single day.

Yes, visualizing counts.
But preparing the way counts twice.
And acting "as if" it's a done deal, seven times.

An enlightened soul
is not one to whom truth has been revealed,
but one who has summoned it. And not just
when they've been driven by pain, but when life's
seas were as calm as glass.

*But you have to admit it's kind of handy that way,
pain. Just worked out like that. Honest.*

Of all the luck!
Can you believe it?

You. In paradise. Now. Exactly as you are.

Exactly as it is.

Do you have any idea how many souls in
the unseen wish they could be in your shoes?
Wish they could see through your eyes?
Wish they could feel what moves in your heart?
Have your friends? Share your loves?
Face your fears and your beasts?

Oh, heck yeah, your fears and your beasts!
Are you kidding? Especially your fears and your
beasts! Because from where they are, it's so much
easier to see how soon they will pass, how
triumphant you will be, and how much
more they'll make possible.

To them,
it's like every day is your birthday.

Haven't you always
found your way?

Hasn't there always been a light in the darkness? Haven't you always gotten back up? Haven't there always been serendipitous surprises, unexpected twists, and triumphant comebacks? And haven't you always had someone to love? Not to mention all of your dreams that have already come true.

Coincidences?
Or maybe, do you think, you, too,
have always been loved?

What a cool month.

What a cool day.

Thoughts, still manifesting,
as predictably as the tides rise.

You, still as free to choose those thoughts,
as the wind blows.

Seems all is well in paradise.

Anything else I can do for you,
anything at all?

Love,
The Universe

*Yeah, right. Sorry. As if something
could beat the power to have it all. Guess I'm just
in one of those silly moods. XXOO*

Think not that today foretells
tomorrow, for it never has.

Same goes for the past.

Only you can do that.

Never forget,

the scorecard that matters most is invisible,
and won't be seen by others until the game is over.
At which point it'll be distributed via our version
of high-def broadband, in 3-D Technicolor,
to everyone you've ever known, and then some.

Of course, all the check boxes will be blank,
except for where you might want to rate yourself
(highly discouraged, by the way), but still, every
single fear you ever faced, every bridge you ever
crossed, and every life you ever touched will be
known and celebrated by all.

*Actually, the party's already started, but it gets
a little bigger every day as the ripples created by your
kindness and courage spread farther and farther.*

Hey, you're HUGE in the unseen.

As much as I love my "job,"
I do have "my days."

Maybe you can help me out?

Tell me, what advice would you give a
child who came to you asking what their
favorite color should be?

That no color is right or wrong? To follow their
heart? That if they wanted to, they could always
change their mind later, any number of times?
That their happiness with their choice is all that
matters? Not to give it too much importance?
That they don't have to decide at all? That you
approve no matter what they choose?

My, you are good!

Now, what if they protested because they
heard from friends that there was a special color
assigned to them at birth, their soul-color.

They felt that a numerology reading might shed some light on their confusion. They wanted confirmation of their choices through a zodiac chart, tea leaves, or a Ouija board. And they asked if finding a new guru would be a good idea.

See?

Sorry to lay that on you. I'm just fishing around for some new answers to the bazillion questions I get each week about careers, loves, and destinies—which to me, from here, are kind of like . . . crayons.

E-w-w-h-h, nice magenta!

Sure, use all the tools, guides, and helpers you like, I approve of them, too, but maybe, reread the fourth paragraph above as well.

It isn't easy at first,
but one of the greatest gifts you could ever
give someone who makes your heart soar is
the freedom to learn their own lessons,
at their own pace.

Even trickier is discovering that one
of the greatest gifts you could ever give someone
who gets on your nerves is the freedom to learn
their own lessons, at their own pace.

And perhaps most challenging of all is
understanding that one of the greatest gifts
you could ever give yourself is understanding that
your heart soaring and your nerves fraying have
never been dependent upon other people
and their lessons.

In all cases, I meant, "besides chocolate."

Pretend you were me.

You're about to create a new reality. And you know you're gonna hang out there, in every imaginable form, for trillions and trillions and trillions of years.

Do you think, just for yucks, you'd build it in such a way that you might get hurt, become less, or not matter?

Or, as the Universe, the alpha and the omega, the bringer of the dawn and each new day, would you be pretty confident that you could craft the most spectacular paradise imaginable? Flawless in every way, yet possessing the odd illusions of pain, loss, and your own irrelevance to heighten suspense, enhance the unknown, and make it one unforgettable, spine-tingling, nonstop adventure that will mean even more to you when you master it again, but from the inside out?

CUT! That's a wrap.

Nice alpha! Were the purple leotards your idea?

XXOO,
The Universe

Don't believe the illusions.

Have you noticed it, too?

How fears are a lot like highway billboards?

The faster you're moving, the quicker they approach, the larger they get, and the more they block your view of what's real and alive. To the point that they tower above you, larger than life itself, giving you pause and more reason than ever to turn around and retreat to safety.

Yet if you muster the courage to stay the course, in just a blink they're behind you, put into proper perspective. And then as quickly as they appeared, they completely vanish.

If you want to stay the course, then please, just stay the course.

That's why we did away with billboards here a long time ago. Besides, no one uses our highways.

Here's the rub.

If it wasn't so flippin' simple—manifesting change,
finding happiness, living the life of your dreams—
I really do think more people would "get it."

Think, think, and let go.

Release me, release me
to do your will. To move heaven and earth.
To orchestrate the players and summon the
circumstances that will change your life completely
by doing your all-out best, with today.

That's all the leg up I need.

Basically, if you can feel it,
I can deal it.

Whatever you want.

With compliments,
The Universe

Emotion summons circumstances.
The greater the emotion,
the greater the circumstances.

Ever wonder what
the world would be like without you?

Who would shine a light into all the dark corners
you now illuminate? Who would comfort, guide,
and inspire all those you now reach? Who would
smile to those who need yours the most?

We do.

All the time.

And it ain't pretty.

Oh, dearie, dearie me . . .
So many claim to believe.

So here's what I'm going to start asking them:
If you really believed you were guided,
wouldn't you begin listening?

And if you really believed you were powerful,
wouldn't every true desire be followed by action?

And if you really believed you could provide the
spark that makes your dreams come true, wouldn't
you stop living as if you weren't sure?

That ought to stir up their coffee, huh?

Let's rock-and-roll.

Be the miracle.

Through you,
through you, through you . . .

The magic works through you. Not beside you.
Not around you. Not for you. Not despite you.
But through you.

You have to go there. You have to choose your
stage. You have to do your dance. Putting yourself
in place, to any degree that you can, even if it
scares you, even when it's "hard," even if it's just
your big toe. Stretch yourself, scoff at the odds,
get the ball rolling so that the magic can then
come alive and sweep you off your feet
with its infinite grace and glory.

You wouldn't just carry around the seeds for
the garden of your dreams in your pocket, all the
while asking where your flowers were? Nope, you'd
have to brave the elements, you'd have to choose
the location, and then you'd have to go there.

Your life is your wand (or hoe, whatever),
The Universe

There will always be something else you could have said. There will always be something else you could have done. And there will always be another life you could have lived.

But, frankly, we're still savoring all you did say, do, and become, in spite of so many reasons that you might not have.

Yeah, "What would [insert your name here] do?" is part of our pop vernacular now. And you should see your pending endorsement deals! Magic carpets, body wands, pixie dust, the works!

Here's a little trick
to get the ball rolling.

Ask yourself, "What's the most fun
I could have with my life, as it is now, before
those big dreams of mine come true?"

Then, do it.

A lot.

The next thing you know,
those big dreams will come true.

*And, if you're not even sure what's fun anymore,
then just do anything. A lot. And it will find you.*

It's that simple.

Your thoughts do become things. Don't fight it.
Don't think there's something else. Don't entertain
the false premises of fate, luck, or a God who judges,
withholds, or decides. You decide. You manifest.
You rule. This is why you're here. This is what
you came to discover. To experience your absolute
dominion over every flimsy, malleable illusion
of time and space. To do, be, and have.

Truthfully, it couldn't be any easier. Not any.
All you have to do is think of what you want,
and not deviate from that thought. Which will
invariably set you in motion, stir up the magic,
and unleash the full force, power, and majesty
of a Universe conspiring on your behalf.

Just do it. It's worth everything you've got.
Be strong, vigilant, and determined,
and the Kingdom of Heaven will appear
at your very feet.

"I got your back."

Now, let's just say

you're a fisher-person, and let's just say
that I've rearranged the stars so that this is
going to be the luckiest week of your life.

Whoohooo!

Tell me, next time you go out on your boat,
will you take one pole, or many?

Many. I thought so.

Would you think, maybe for the glimmering
of a moment, that as a lucky person, you won't
have to fish anymore, because the fish will
come to you?

No. Probably not. You've always been one
of the sharper tools in the shed.

So tell me, why is it so easy for most to see that
with luck, even, they still have to put themselves
out there, and that the more they do, the greater
the yield. Yet when it comes to life's magic,
thoughts becoming things, and the Universe
conspiring on their behalf, they think
their fish will come to them?

Your first mate, always,
The Universe

*No, there's no such thing as luck. Just folks who believe
in the magic enough to fish at every opportunity.*

Do you know what
you've created?

No, besides an intergallactically
known saunter named after you.

Inspiration, in the eyes that have watched you.
Hope, in the minds that have admired you.
And love, in the hearts that have known you.

Not bad, kiddo, not bad at all.

*But you might ease up on your sashay
before someone gets hurt.*

Here's some advice for those
who come to you with long faces.

"If you've finally decided, once and for all,
to be happy, yet you aren't . . . then you haven't
yet decided to be happy, once and for all."

Same goes for all the other stuff they've decided.

They're that powerful.

*Always being your best, shining your brightest,
and standing as tall as you can, pays far more
dividends than one might ever imagine.*

Don't you marvel at nature?
I do, but then I'm partial.

It holds so many clues about living the life of your dreams, don't you think?

For instance, have you ever seen a mama duck waiting around for her ducklings to line up before crossing the street?

Never. Because she knows that the only way her ducklings are ever going to line up is if she first starts out on a new adventure.

Just one of your ducks,
The Universe

*It's the same for your ducks,
they won't line up, either, until you start.*

New Soul Orientation

The following words and phrases are not in
my vocabulary: "Should." "Difficult." "Evil."
"I don't know."

Oh sure, there'll be plenty of times you can
use them, and everyone will know exactly what
you mean—especially me—at which point all
the elements will conspire to make them
true for you.

I also never ask, "How?"
Might as well just ask, "What Universe?"

Dismissed,
This Universe

Oh, and there's one more. "Good-bye."
It's a bit of fiction that totally tears me up.

Sometimes the suspense here
becomes almost too much.

Like right now.

Before you, in the unseen,
there are some amazing, mind-blowing
circumstances now brewing.

Wheels are turning, fires are burning,
and all possibilities are being recalculated.

Players, player-ettes, and accomplices
are lining up, soon to burst into your life.

All just waiting for the nod from me . . .
as I wait for the nod from you.

Wha-Hu-Ha! This is so much fun!

Once you know, commit and never look back.

Best friends may tell you
what to do. Yep, because that's
what best friends do.

Wise friends, however, wouldn't dream of it
because they understand that they'll never
know of all the secrets that stir in your heart,
of your gifts that lie in waiting, or of the plans
that we have made.

S-h-h-h-h-h,
The Universe

And I'm not telling.

One hundred trillion years!

7 continents!

106 billion people!
(not counting Atlantis, and the others)

96 zillion dreams manifested!

And not once, not even close, not even on
my most generous, loving, caring days, has anything
ever happened in time and space—good or bad,
big or small, rich or poor—that wasn't sparked
by someone's imagination and followed up with
their own baby steps.

Now remind me, what is it you most want?

Not without you,
The Universe

Pssst . . . Hey, gorgeous!

Want to know a secret?

Everything in your life is a symbol.

A reflection. A clue. A reminder.

Of what you understand,
and of what you don't, made manifest.

Look to the beauty for truth.
And to what hurts, for its beauty.

*Oh, yes indeed, life is fair. As fair as it is beautiful.
Though this can't always be seen from too close, in
terms of either time or space.*

Happily . . .

Between here and there,
the only thing that matters is what
you think between now and then.

*The past is simply what you choose to remember,
if you even choose to remember it.*

Ever pour cement?

Heavy stuff, but it's a simple job. Just mix, set, and leave it alone. You can even make shapes out of it, like ducks, flowers, or figurines, depending on the mold. There's no limit.

Now, let's just say that you don't like the way a particular duck came out. Would you try to repour or manipulate the cast concrete, or would you simply start over, considering that cement is dirt cheap?

Oh, you're way ahead of me! You saw that "mix, set, and leave" was like a metaphor for using your imagination, didn't you? You also got that the mold is your goal or dream. I think the "no limit" tipped you off, too. "Heavy stuff," "simple," and "cheap" were also clues. But what I'm most proud of is that you saw how repouring or manipulating cast concrete is like trying to effect change in one's life by tweaking what's already manifested, instead of going within and manifesting anew.

Five Gold Stars for you today,
The Universe

If you knew of a spectacular mountain that was very, very tall, yet climbable, and if it was well established that from its peak you could literally see all the love that bathes the world, dance with the angels, and party with the "Gods," would you curse, or celebrate, each step you took as you ascended it?

Right-o. Life is that mountain, and each day a step.

Have no fear.
Last time I checked, you were so close to the top they were taking your toga measurements.

Has it struck you yet
that answers come before questions?
That healing begins with illness? And that
you can't have a dream come true without
a time when it hasn't?

Shoot, isn't it all so perfect? Everyone, no matter
where they are on their journey, can be happy.

*At all times, and in all matters,
everything is happening in your favor.*

Please, don't be afraid.

Not even a little. Not ever. The lions and tigers and bears can't really hurt you. You live in a world of fog and mirrors where there's only the illusion that you could somehow become less than the greatest you've ever imagined yourself to be.

And it's this very image, the highest from within you, that has summoned your boldest dreams, daring you into the light with their sweet rewards and drawing you through the very fears that have kept you from it.

Slayer of dragons. Matador of all time and space. Rightful heir to heaven on earth. Don't be afraid. Not even a little.

Amen,
The Universe

I guess I just needed to blog.

You're not here to learn
how to make your thoughts become the things
and events of your life. Too hard, too complicated.
B-o-r-i-i-i-n-g. Leave this to me.

No, you're here to learn that they already do.
Every single one of them.
Always have, always will.

How could it be easier?

Imagine yourself
on a warm summer evening before a calm,
clear pond. The moon is full. The stars are shining.
Whippoorwills are whippoor-willing.

And I am with you.

Now, do you know how to float on water? For the
most part you do absolutely nothing, at which point
I can hold you at the surface, in the palm of my
hand. It's simply a matter of physics, the laws of
time and space, and your natural state.

Are you with me?

Okay, now you'll have to trust me, but it's the same when it comes to floating in wealth and abundance, health and harmony, friends and laughter. These are your natural state, your default settings, the "givens" in this great adventure. These are where true balance is found. They can be yours without strenuous effort. You don't even have to visualize them. Just stop the argument that claims you're without. Surrender in the war that presumes lack. Come out from the fort that has kept you so safe, and follow your heart with abandon.

It's as if, when moving
from point A to point B in your life—
from sickness to health, poverty to wealth,
whatever—at some point in the journey,
arriving at point B becomes inevitable,
a sure thing. However, at no point in
your journey is this physically verifiable—
until you reach point B.

The point being (yuck, yuck), you may
have already crossed that line.
But you'll never know it,
unless you see the journey through.

Time and space, what a hoot.
Look to them for answers, direction,
and meaning, and they'll rock your
world every which way.

Yet discover that they look to *you*
for answers, direction, and meaning,
and *you* will rock the world.

Take my word for it,
the latter is your "ticket."

Tallyho, maestro—

The Universe

*What an adventure,
if I do say so myself.*

Ooh! Ooh! Ooh!

Have I mentioned that everyone
knows exactly what you're thinking?

How else could you draw new friends
from the unseen? How else would your heroes,
heroines, and scoundrels know when to appear,
or move on? How else would your "stars"
get their cues?

True, they think their own thoughts, too.
How else would you know who to cast
in each scene?

Just thinking of you,
and your power to choose.

Yikes . . . even those thoughts!

Everything can change
so very, very fast.

And it usually does.

Whoohoooooooooo!

Imagine . . .

You're sitting upon your throne overlooking your Kingdom (Queendom, whatever 'dom you like), and masses upon masses of people surround you in throngs.

They're cheering your name, laying flowers at your feet, and imploring you to join them in the village where they've prepared a feast to celebrate your life.

You humbly accept their invitation, and immediately you're whisked off your feet and lifted high upon the shoulders of your joyful admirers, thoroughly overwhelmed by their heartfelt gratitude and desire to please you.

Midway through the most extravagant party you've ever attended, amid laughter and happy tears, you begin reflecting on your life and in no way can you recall what you've done to deserve such an outpouring of love.

Suddenly embarrassed, and wondering if you aren't dreaming the whole thing, you turn to a member of your entourage and whisper in her ear, "Are you sure there hasn't been some kind of mistake? I mean, I don't even recall having a Kingdom! Who are all these people? Who do they think I am?"

And she whispers back, "There's no mistake. They know exactly who you are. These are just some of the souls whose lives had reached a fork in the road, as most lives do, where hope and despair had met, and because of something you said or did—directly or indirectly—they were, as you might say, shown the way, reborn, and, eventually, able to shine their light onto the paths of others in need. That's who they are, and in case you haven't noticed, more keep arriving in a procession that will never end.

And no, this isn't a dream."

And no, again. I didn't say "thongs."
But I'd imagine that could be arranged.

If it was just about surviving,
getting by, and keeping things the way they are,
then how would you explain imagination?

If it was just about sacrifice, selflessness, and
altruism, then how would you explain desire?

And if it was just about thinking, reflecting,
and spiritual stuff, then how would you
explain the physical world?

Want it all.
That's what it, and you, are there for.

Vroom, vroom,
The Universe

You could call me your friend,
but that's not quite enough.
You could call me your guide,
but there's more to it than that.

You could call me your conspirator, your helper,
or your agent; your coach, counselor, or confidant;
your father, mother, or child. You could call me
the sun, the moon, and the stars; the wind,
the sky, and the rain; the past, the present,
and the future.

But really, what I'm getting at, the purpose behind
all these Notes, and perhaps what I'd most like to
hear one day, is you calling me "yourself."

O-h-m-m-m-m-m . . .

Just as I've always called you "myself."
(With unimaginable pride, I might add.)